Kind, Curious, and Crafty: a sad girl's guide to living a happy life

Carrie Polynkin

BookLeaf Publishing

Presentation by *BookLeaf Publishing*

Web: www.bookleafpub.com

E-mail: info@bookleafpub.com

ISBN: 9789395755702

First edition 2022

For T & J, my whole entire world

and for Ryder, who I miss terribly.

ACKNOWLEDGEMENT

This book of poetry wouldn't have been possible if it weren't for the loves of my life. My mother, who has always stood by my side and believed in me when I didn't believe in myself. My father, whose quiet comfort and headstrong determination has always inspired me. My grandparents, all of whom worked hard to build a life of love and sincerity and stability. My step parents and my in-laws, who came into my life and taught me the meaning of family. To my siblings, who really know me, the true me, the me I often hid away. My friends, who accepted me for who I was and not who I thought I should have been. To my extended family, of whom there are many - all loved and appreciated by this oddball. You have always made me feel accepted and welcome and loved.

And to my husband, my other half and perfect match. Who built a life with me filled with love and laughter and true happiness. To whom I am eternally grateful for.

But most importantly, my two boys. Who marked the beginning of my life, who brought with them into the world whole pieces of my heart, and who I would never be able to live without.

And of course, to Book Leaf Publishing, for challenging me and inspiring me to do something I never thought I could do.

Thank you. I love you all. Even you, Book Leaf.

PREFACE

I am not a poet. I have never considered myself a poet. I have never even considered myself capable of writing poetry. Or at least, not poetry that anyone would want to read. Then again, most of my life I haven't felt capable. Which is quite sad to be honest. I have spent almost the entirety of my life trying to be happy. Trying to be content. Trying to fit myself in a box. And it wasn't until I took myself out of that box, that I was truly able to find the happiness that I was so desperately searching for.

This challenge scared me. I didn't think I would be able to do it. I thought, in underestimating myself, I would be less disappointed when my premonition proved true. I wouldn't be surprised to know that I was a failure, I knew I was going to fail going into this. But then something changed in me. I decided to take a chance on myself. I decided to do the unthinkable and actually believe in myself.

These poems may not be earth shattering, but I wrote them from my heart. Some of them rhyme, some don't. Some make sense, some don't. But at the end of the day, I did something that scared me and I did it my way. I wrote these poems for myself and for people like me. For dreamers. For romantics. For people who don't consider themselves poets. For people who look in the mirror and don't love the person they see staring back.

I challenge you to change your mind about yourself. I'm thirty years old and just now coming to the conclusion that I may not be half bad. Heck, I might even like myself.

BE KIND

life is hard
but you don't have to be
there is enough hardness
here already

you can be kind
start small if you must
one kind word
even just to yourself

it might not catch
like the fervid wildfire
instead it is a drop of rain
not enough but a start

FIND JOY IN EVERY DAY

some days aren't great
I'll be the first to admit that
but some days
the sun rises so red against the ocean
and the clouds paint the sky in vivid colours
and the wind blows against your cheek
and everything feels ok

some days aren't great
I've had many not great days
but some days
the grocery store has everything you need
and the things you love are all on sale
and the isles are clear
and the radio is playing all your favourite songs
and things aren't ok, but for a moment
it feels fine

some days aren't great
they're boring or they're annoying
your plans were foiled and your friends
let you down
but it's a full moon
and the stars shine the brightest they've ever
shone

and it's cool and it's calm
and for the tiniest moment
even though it's just a moment
it's all ok

some days aren't great
some days are pure misery
and on those days it's ok
to not be ok

some days aren't great
but some days are
and you have to hold on to those great days
and on the not great days
on the miserable days
try to find one tiny piece of joy

and if you can't
try again tomorrow

because some days aren't great
and some days are

BE YOUR AUTHENTIC SELF

I am the only me
as you're the only you
it may sound so cliche
but it is also true

it took a lot of years
for me to finally realize
I tried to be so many people
but it was right before my eyes

I am the only me
this is all i've got
I have to learn to love me
or I'll end up living not

I looked into the mirror
I frowned at what I saw
it wasn't much to work with
when i should have been in awe

for a tiny moment
I decided to pretend
I'd act like I was happy
and treat her like a friend

she is actually quite beautiful
in an unconventional way
her eyes are kind and playful
and she makes me want to stay

her stance is so unsure
so I straighten up my back
her smile lights up her face
and she soon starts to relax

she's funny and she's bold
in unexpected ways
she loves her people fiercely
and she's happy when she plays

she tells the kind of jokes
that make you roll your eyes
her laugh fills the room
she is quirky and she's wise

I decided then to like her
despite my predisposition
it took years for me to make it
but it was the right decision

I am the only me
and you are the only you
I'm sure if you give yourself the chance
you would like you too

MAKE TIME

what if you only had today
to do everything you wanted to do
would you be able to do it
or would you go to bed tonight, disappointed
longing for one more day
perhaps tomorrow
perhaps tomorrow would be a better day
or the tomorrow after that
what happens when your tomorrows run out
will you do everything you wanted to do
or will you go to bed disappointed

DON'T LET THE DARKNESS WIN

tw: depression, suicide

I am not made out of sunshine
as I may claim to be
I am like so many others
there is darkness in me

the shadow on my life
the pain I carried in my ways
it stole away my years
it took so many days

an overwhelming empty
a terrifying guilt
a shame no one should carry
the house that darkness built

in my darkest moments
I didn't think I'd stay alive
made a deal with my best friend
that we'd both see 25

the darkness lived within me
extinguishing my light
it stole away my memories
I couldn't win the fight

it took a lot of faith
and it was hard to see
but eventually I fought to find
my way back to being me

it still lives in me now
though I've found some ways to cope
I live my days more fully now
my life is filled with hope

at the end of all the darkness,
that's where life can begin
if there is one thing I know
it's that you cannot let it win

CREATE

what were we put here for?
and by whom and when and how
our existence is a mystery
one that I'll let lay for now

what makes us any different
than the birds up in the sky
than the fish that swim the oceans
or the silver wolves that cry

I can ask so many questions
I may never know the truth
yes patience is a virtue
that is wasted on the youth

it's much too much to handle
to carry this heavy weight
there is one thing that is for certain
we were put here to create

DON'T COMPARE
YOURSELF TO OTHERS

to the to the fish the bird might have it all
a wide open sky, space to to fly
but the bird will never know
the feeling of cool water on thirsty gills, the
beauty of the depth in the darkness,
the comfort of a school tight beside you

to the housecat the wild animal might have it all
the freedom to roam, a lifetime of adventure
but the wild animal will never know
the peaceful luxury of living indoors, the warm
security of a bed to sleep in
the gentle touch of a loving hand on his back

to the winter the summer might have it
all the warmth of the sun, the long bright days
but the summer will never know
the beauty of the snowflake
falling so delicate, fragile
on a crisp cold winter morning

to the day the night might have it all
dark, mysterious, exotic
but the night will never know

the captivating sunrise
full of longing, anticipation
bringing the sense of a fresh beginning

to you someone else might have it all
but their things are not you
there are things that you have that they will
never know
there are parts of your life that they can only
dream of

like the fish
the house cat
the winter
the night

you might have all that you need

AND DON'T GIVE A DAMN WHAT THEY THINK

have you ever danced like no one was watching
truly, freely, with no hesitation
have you ever sang like no one was listening
out of tune, top of your lungs,
really really singing
it's easy to say these things
it's easy to pretend that we would do it
but deep down I'm not sure
I don't see many people dancing
I don't hear many people singing

have you ever lived like you had no expectations
like you could do whatever you wanted
like you could truly live the way you truly want
to live
terrifying right
what would they think if you're really lived
sang
danced
laughed
dressed
exactly how you wanted to

if you called yourself whatever name
if you wore whatever clothing
if you lived wherever you wanted

what would they think
what would happen if you didn't care what they
thought
truly didn't care
You could live freely, openly
 completely untethered by the expectations of
someone else

what then

FIND YOUR PEOPLE

you are not for everyone
you can never be
but for some people
you are everything

the most important thing
you can do in this life
is find your people
and love them right

you can't be for everyone
everyone isn't for you
but some people
will be your everything

ALLOW YOURSELF TO
FALL IN LOVE

I've always been a romantic
it's a fatal flaw of mine
I saw the good in everyone
the potential for a future
because I could make anything work
and in this sad optimism
I didn't realize that I was holding myself back
from the future I needed to create for myself

so for a long time
I didn't want to believe in love
I didn't want to get hurt again
I didn't want to depend on anyone else

I thought I knew everything
I thought I had seen every colour
but until I knew you
I didn't even know what I didn't know

I've fallen in love a hundred times
with the same pair of eyes
you've given me more than you'll ever know

if I hadn't taken the risk

if I hadn't let myself fall
I can't imagine where I'd be now

I've always been a romantic
but there's something different about this kind of
love
it's a full love
a contentment that I didn't think I deserved
a happiness that fills my bones and lightens my
footsteps
it makes me see all the colours a little bit
brighter
it's the sappy kind of love that some people hate

but if you allow yourself to fall
you might find yourself hating it a little less

BE CURIOUS

17

there is so much we don't know
so many songs we haven't heard
so many things we haven't seen

there are infinite possibilities in this life
a thousand things you can be
a million choices you get to make

what can happen if you open up your heart
to the endless possibilities that lay before you
aren't you curious

TREAT YOUR BODY WELL

how old were you
when you learned to hate your body

were you one
toddling for the first time, taking your first big
steps into the world
surely you didn't hate your body then
your body was amazing then

were you four
going to school for the first time
eager to learn, excited to make friends
wearing a cute little outfit that your mom picked
out
a little pink sweater
you couldn't have hated your body then
you looked amazing in that sweater

were you ten
when life got heavy and complicated
the people you loved leaving and fighting
fighting and leaving
did you hate your body then
your body did nothing wrong then

were you fifteen
when you started noticing boys and girls
but boys and girls didn't seem to notice you
was there something about your body
that was unnoticeable to them
did you hate your body then

were you eighteen
falling in love for the first time
real love, the kind that devastates you

were you nineteen
going off in the world alone for the first time
alone and lonely in the hardest ways

were you twenty
when you realized that everything you wanted
was everything you couldn't have

is that when you learned to hate your body?

how old were you
when you learned to hate your body
and how old will you be
when you learn how wrong you were

to hate a body that carried you through
some of the hardest moments of your life

and in your greatest moments
it was that same body that housed you

how old were you when you learned to hate your
body
and how old will you be when you unlearn

HELP THOSE IN NEED

it's so easy
to lend a helping hand
when life is good
and things are easy

but to help someone in need
when you are in need too
that's a special kind of love
given by the most special kind of person

there are so many people in this world
that need a little bit of kindness
a steady hand to hold them as they stand
a little bit of hope amidst their darkness

you might be one of those people
and you might have been one of those people
I certainly have
and I will be again

and in those moments
where you don't feel strong enough to help yourself
help someone else

I promise you it will heal you in unexpected ways

AND ASK FOR HELP
WHEN YOU NEED IT

if helping is healing
and we can all use some of that
asking for help
is an extension

then why is it so difficult to ask
when we need something
reaching out feels like an impossibility
at least, that's how it is for me

I'd rather struggle through it
than let someone know I'm struggling
I'd rather fight my own fight
when someone could so easily win it for me

I don't ask for help, it's not in my nature
I know it's not healthy
I know I need help sometimes
but I can't bring myself to stoop

something so embarrassing about having issues
so silly to struggle
why am I so ashamed to be human
why can't I admit that I can't do it all

helping is healing
I help wherever I can, whenever I'm able
but to ask?
no, never, I can't do that

I know I'm only human
I have many flaws, I'll never deny that
but I don't ask for help
not from anyone, not at any time

if I can't take care of it myself
I shouldn't have the opportunity
I don't deserve the challenge
I don't know why I can't ask for help

I'm learning to be better
I try now, at least I try
I'm trying to ask when I need it
promise me you'll do the same

DREAM BIG, LITTLE ONE

how different would your life be
if you life turned out exactly like you wanted it
to
when you were six years old
when you thought you could do anything

how many dreams did you have
that you lost through the years
slipped away through your fingers
like soap washing down the drain

why did you stop dreaming
when did you learn to limit your own desires
what made you change your mind about yourself
how could things be different

when we are young we're told to dream big
constantly and by everyone
while secretly they stopped dreaming
for themselves a long time ago

but why
why do we stop dreaming
when do we decide on that complacency
when do we stop believing in ourselves

and those that do dare to keep dreaming
past the invariably determined limit
are considered lost and listless
or vain and reckless

I will dream for as long as I sleep
and as long as I wake
I will strive for that life that I dreamed of
when I was six years old

and it may never come
but it won't be because I didn't try
because I really took it to heart when they said
"dream big, little one"

HOPE FOR THE BEST,
EXPECT THE BEST

what careless optimism is this
to expect the best for yourself
when everything around you makes you feel
like you don't deserve what you want

I was always wary of expectations
afraid that I would disappoint myself further
if I set myself up like that
so I stayed vigilant, no anticipation

if you are ready for disappointment
it won't hurt as badly
it won't wound you
like it would if you weren't expecting it

it's easier to protect yourself
from the disenchantment all around us
but imagine the magic
of allowing yourself to hope for the best

because you do deserve the best
and I wish the best for you
and I hope you learn to wish the best for yourself
because though the fall is higher the view is
remarkable

DON'T LET THEM SEE
YOU SWEAT

confidence is key
that's what they always say
fake it til you make it
I guess that's the only way

more cliches and lameness
feel free to roll your eyes
but believe me when I tell you
it worked, to my surprise

before I was afraid
nervous about a beginning
but take that chance and do it
I promise you'll be winning

pretend you're doing well
act like you're unafraid
set your mind to do it
and soon you'll have it made

so take on any challenge
and don't let yourself forget
whatever it is you do
don't ever let them see you sweat

SHOW UP

I am a hider
I have hidden away so many times in my life
from jobs, from friends
opportunities
all passed by
hiding
often under the covers of my bed
so many days I spent under those covers
ignoring phone calls
keeping the curtains closed
terrified to face the outside world
and the longer I hid, the worse things got
but still I hid

I'm tying now to hide less
I still hide at times
I'm not perfect but I try
I try not to dwell on the past
usually I don't
but sometimes I wonder what would have happened
if I didn't hide
how many opportunities passed me by
how many friends left me behind
who I would have become
if I had only showed up

GET CRAFTY

don't let them put you in a box
no one survives in a box for long
hold on to the things that make you you
hold on for dear life and never let go
when things get tough
always remember that you are tougher
you are capable of magic
you are made of stardust
look at yourself in the mirror and allow yourself
to love your reflection
to accept who you are
to be proud of your accomplishments
don't be afraid to do things that scare you
be unapologetically yourself
you are worthy of love
you are worthy of greatness
you are limitless
defy the odds
surpass your own expectations
believe in yourself
love yourself

I believe in you
I love you
I'm in your corner always

you can do anything
and if all else fails

get crafty